Mou

Life on this side of the mountain

Introduction

'My sheep hear my voice, and I know them, and they follow me'. (John 10:27)

All Christians have the ability to hear the voice of God. The fact that you have heard the voice of God at least once is the definition of what it means to be a Christian. All Christians have experienced a moment when something inside clicked. The light bulb turned on and you forever believed that there is a God and that Jesus Christ is God incarnate.

To some, the moment came as they listened to a speaker. To some, it was as they were reading a book. To some, it was a dramatic or even traumatic event in their life. For whatever the reason, the epiphany occurred and their belief system was changed forever.

The amount of drama associated with such an event is not as important as the lasting impact it makes on the person's life. Sure, everyone likes a dramatic story. But the real miracle is in how the event fundamentally changes the person going forward.

I believe that in many ways the moment after such a moment is of more importance than the moment itself. The moment after the moment can determine your belief system for the rest of your life. If you believed that you reached your epiphany on your own, then you are likely to become a humanist, believing mainly in the power of the human intellect. If, however, you believe that your new found enlightenment came from God, then this hopefully set you on a path of learning about and discovering the God behind the revelation, the God who has shown Himself much bigger and wiser than yourself. Since you are reading this (Christian) book, you most likely fall into the latter category.

The human intellect is certainly capable of great things. God has given it the ability to imagine and learn amazing things, which includes learning about the nature of God. Through reading God-inspired books and through the study of Church history, you can clearly trace the interaction of God in the affairs of men and learn much about the nature of God. But the human intellect has its limitations. People learn by associating new information with old. Such association gives the information context. To remember a fact, people need to categorize it.

Receiving revelation creates entirely new categories.

I pray this book brings revelation. I pray this book causes you to spend time contemplating God, who is the giver of all revelation.

Throughout our lives we learning through our five physical senses: taste, touch, hearing, seeing and smelling. Through them we come to learn about the physical world around us. Evidence about the existence of God abounds in the physical but to truly get to know the person of God, we need to learn to use our spiritual senses.

The journey of discovering God is a journey of revelation. Revelation comes as we exercise our spiritual senses. We must learn to see the hand of God in events around us. We must learn to hear His voice guiding and directing our path. I am constantly being blown away as God reveals Himself to me. I believe that we will spend eternity having God constantly creating new categories.

As it is true in the natural, so it is true in the spiritual, all new information, all new knowledge must have an external source. In the physical, that source can be simply the world around us or it can be another person. The information can be transferred either directly (in person) or indirectly (through a book or recording). In the spirit, true revelation can come directly from God or indirectly through God inspired words. It is on God, the source of all revelation that we must stay our focus. It is God who enlightens. It is God who gives revelation.

This book is about mountains. Mountains are where men go hoping to hear the voice of God. This book contains lessons, keys to hearing the voice of God. Our God is a speaking God. His voice will come in many ways: in thoughts, in images, in feelings, in intuition. You need to learn to recognize when it is God who is speaking to you. Once you learn to recognize the voice of God, your entire life will change.

Developing the ability to recognize the voice of God is a process, which starts with the belief that God has and will continue to speak to you on a very personal level. Once you really believe this to be true, once you have faith, then you will start to recognize His gentle voice more frequently. You will start to recognize His subtle nudges as you walk through your day. Eventually, you will come to know His ever speaking presence in the person of the Holy Spirit in your life.

Valleys

Before we contemplate mountains, we need to spend a little time learning how God works in valleys. To have mountains, there must be valleys. I love mountain tops. I love my times with God when He gives me glimpses of the grand picture of my life. Those visions impart the direction that sustains me day to day. But to get to mountain tops you must first learn to walk in valleys.

When God started to press upon me the topic of this book (about mountains and hearing the voice of God), He immediately called me to meditate again on the topic of repentance. Repentance is a foundational principle of Christianity. It is a topic that I studied at length during my first years of being a Christian. But, lately God has radically changed how I view repentance. I no longer associate repentance with spiritual/emotional 'low' times in my life.

Hebrews 6:1-3:

Therefore, leaving the discussion of the elementary principles of Christ, let us go on to perfection, not laying again the foundation of repentance from dead works and of faith toward God, 2 of the doctrine of baptisms, of laying on of hands, of resurrection of the dead, and of eternal judgment. 3 And this we will do if God permits.

When most people think of repentance, they think about their initial conversion experience. They (rightly) define repentance as a change of heart, a change of direction given by God, the result being a turning away from their prior worldly/sinful life path to a new God-oriented path. They speak of repentance in the past tense. "I've repented from my sin".

All Christians have repentance as the starting point of their journey with God. It is a big part of your past. It needs also to be a big part of your present. What you must learn is that repentance is the key to being transformed into the image of God. Repentance is how God transforms from us 'from glory to glory' (2 Corinthians 3:18). It is the continuous process by which He transforms the lives of His children.

Let me illustrate.

In this fallen world, all of us experience disappointment. You need to start viewing disappointment as a God ordained opportunity for change to occur. God actually allows disappointment so that we grow in godliness. Such growth comes about by the way we learn to respond to disappointment.

Disappointment creates a need to be comforted. The unsaved man will respond to that need by turning to the world or to their own self effort. As Christians, we must learn to turn instead to God.

We all at times will experience disappointment; in people, in places, in activities. Disappointment happens when reality does not match up to our preconceived ideas and expectations. We bring such expectations into every situation. When disappointment happens, we need to learn to turn to the Holy Spirit (not to other things) for our comfort. The role of the Holy Spirit is to comfort and to teach you. He is able to comfort, to heal and to transform how you view your disappointing experience. He will teach you to see things from God's perspective.

Here's the 'expectation cycle' we are born with ...

Expectation -> Reality -> Disappointment -> Need for Comfort ->
Turning to yourself/world for Comfort -> Worldly Expectations for the Future

God wants to change your expectation cycle to ...

Expectation -> Reality -> Disappointment -> Need for Comfort ->
Turning to God for Comfort -> Godly Expectations for the Future

Here's the great part: as you allow God to give you godly expectations. These godly expectations will match future reality! Disappointment will become a rare event. When it does happen to occur, the Holy Spirit will take the opportunity to quickly give you God's perspective. This is the process by which the Holy Spirit transforms you into the image of God. Your view of the world around you will change, event by event, into God's view of the world.

God wants to give you His heavenly perspective. Repentance is the key to growing in that perspective.

Repentance starts with being humble enough to allow God to change how you view things. It starts with you acknowledging that your views are incomplete and imperfect and then asking God for the gift of His perfect/complete view.

God never fails to give His perfect view.

By His mercy, God gives His perfect view a little at a time. I say, by His mercy, because we only can handle transformation a little at a time. Like layers of an onion, His is peeling away the falsehood taught by the world and replacing it with His truth. This is the divine working out of our salvation. (Philippians 2:12) This is divine revelation. It comes from continually humbling ourselves before God, acknowledging our views are lacking and receiving His point of view. His response is always gentle. God is always loving and kind. He always answers.

The expectations that you carry will change over time. Your expectations at the end of the 'expectation cycle' will be different than what you carried into the situation. Your expectations are based upon your views of reality. God has shown me six such views that are the keys to your spiritual growth. The views are: God and the World, Yourself and Others, Your Past and Your Future.

Your View of God

How do you view God? I do some prayer counseling and this is always one of the first questions I ask. Do you perceive Him as your comforter, friend or father? Of course, God is Holy Spirit, Jesus and Father. So, any of these answers is correct. The question has to do with the kind of relationship you have with God. It says a lot about your view of God. It also will have a bearing on the kind of relationships you have or don't have with others.

Is God near or distance? Is He close by or far away? Do you feel His presence? If God seems far away, then this is an issue that needs to be addressed. One name of God is 'Emanuel' which means 'God with us' (Matthew 1:23). The names of God reveal His divine attributes. It is always God's desire to be near. But His gentleness, His kindness is such that He never forces Himself on anyone.

James 4:8:

Draw near to God and He will draw near to you.
Cleanse your hands, you sinners; and
purify your hearts, you double-minded. Lament and
mourn and weep! Let your laughter be turned to
mourning and your joy to gloom. Humble yourselves in the
sight of the Lord, and He will lift you up.

Your view of God needs to be transformed from a view of someone who is distance and uncaring to a view of an intimate loving Father, Mother and Friend. When Christ is in you, God Himself is inside of you. God cannot be any closer.

In Him we live and move and have our being (Acts 17:28). We are literally swimming in God. This is the mystery that has been hid from ages and from generations. (Colossians 1:27)

With that said, different people perceive God differently. Also, that perspective will change during different periods of one's life. As I mentioned, to some He is comforter (Holy Spirit), to some good friend (Jesus) and to some protector and advisor (Father). At different times it is normal for one or more of the three persons of the trinity to be more closely perceived.

In the process of daily repentance, we can see the roles played by each person of the trinity. For the comfort needed when reality falls short of expectations, for life's disappointments, you need to learn to allow the Holy Spirit to comfort you. Allow the bear hug of God to happen. It takes your consent. It requires you becoming as a little child seeking the embrace of your heavenly parent.

Micah 6:8:

He has shown you, O man, what is good and what does the LORD require of you. But to do justly,
To love mercy, And to walk humbly with your God?

Once you learn to walk humbly with God, once you admit your need and allow yourself to be comforted, the Holy Spirit will proceed in guiding you and leading you into all truth.

John 16:13:

However, when He, the Spirit of truth, has come, <u>He will guide you into all truth</u>; for He will not speak on His own authority, but whatever He hears He will speak; and He will tell you things to come. (My Underline)

Notice that the Holy Spirit will not only be your guide in life, but he will also change your expectation of the future! He will let you know what to expect as you listen for His voice concerning future situations. I have found this to be especially true immediately after disappointing situations. At such times, stop and listen for the voice of God. You will hear His voice as you cry out to Him for comfort.

His voice will be the voice of comfort and rational perspective. Ignore the accusatory voice of recrimination. Satan is the 'accuser of our brothers' (Revelation 12:10) One voice will bring you peace. One will not. Turn away from evil. Seek peace and pursue it. (1 Peter 3:11)

Salvation is the Great Thought of God

We need to change our view of God. One way to do this is to consider salvation from a Biblical perspective. It is God's desire for all men to be saved and to come to knowledge of the truth. (2 Peter 3:9)

Your salvation was God's idea. He was thinking about you long before you ever gave Him a thought.

Jeremiah 31:34:

No more shall every man teach his neighbor, and every man his brother, saying, 'Know the LORD,' for they all shall know Me, from the least of them to the greatest of them, says the LORD. For I will forgive their iniquity, and their sin I will remember no more.

I've been a Christian for some time. I still need to frequently remind myself of the great goodness of God. All of us need to soak in the picture of God painted in the Bible, letting it change our view of God. Meditate on the following scriptures. Allow them to change your view of God.

Psalm 42:8:

The LORD will command His loving-kindness in the daytime,
And in the night His song shall be with me—
A prayer to the God of my life.

God is not some impersonal, judgmental lightning bolt thrower. God is good all the time. He is for you, not against you. He wants the best for your life. He created you and wants you to be fulfilled. His song should fill your life. His joy should fill your life.

Psalm 40:11:

Do not withhold Your tender mercies from me, O LORD;
Let Your loving-kindness and Your truth continually
preserve me.

According to His tender mercies, God blots out your
transgressions. (Psalm 51:1) All of His actions are
motivated by His loving-kindness. His covenants are
motivated by His love. Scriptures are not to be viewed as
lists of dos and don'ts. They are the advice of a loving
Father who wants the best for you.

Psalm 103:4:

Who redeems your life from destruction,
Who crowns you with loving-kindness and tender mercies

How much does God love you? He gave His only son to
redeem your life from destruction. So much of religion is
built around trying to please God, when really it should be
simply a celebration of the fact that He already loves us
beyond comprehension.

Psalm 107:43:

Whoever is wise will observe these things,
And they will understand the loving-kindness of the LORD.

My life's quest is to know the Lord. And so, my first
priority every day is spending time with the Lord. When I
do, I learn to observe things as gifts from the Lord. I allow
things to be a constant reminder of His loving-kindness.
Then when others are not kind, their actions simply

remind me of how kind God really is. When others do not love, their indifference only puts the great love of God in stark contrast.

Jeremiah 9:24:

But let him who glories glory in this, That he understands and knows Me,
That I *am* the LORD, exercising loving-kindness, judgment, and righteousness in the earth.
For in these I delight," says the LORD.

Your View of the World

The second view of reality that needs to be changed is your view of the world and your place in it.

As a Christian, you are a spiritual being who is being blessed by your father with the experience of living in the physical world. You need to view your time here as a gift. Your family, your friends, your home (no matter how humble), yes even your job are all gifts from God.

Being unthankful is a sin. It comes from taking your eyes off of God and judging by worldly standards.

We see around us today the result of people angry that others are being blessed. Be happy when God blesses others. Also be careful when you are blessed by God, for with a gift comes the responsibility of being a good steward of what He has given you.

Be content with what God has given you.

1 Corinthians 10:12:

For we dare not class ourselves or compare ourselves with those who commend themselves. But they, measuring themselves by themselves, and comparing themselves among themselves, are not wise.

If you feel disappointed with what you have here on earth, that disappointment should be a prompt for you to allow God to show you your home in heaven.

In one respect you should be a little disappointed with this life because it does not compare with the glory waiting for you in heaven. Yet, as you allow the Holy Spirit to change your heart regarding the things of this earth, He will allow you to see the hand of God in every person, place and thing in your life. Seek His eternal perspective concerning things of this earth. Let Him show you their beauty and place in His creation. As He changes your heart you will see things in a different light.

The key for having a transformed world view is spending time with God. Share every aspect of your life with God. Wait on Him and He will give you His perspective. Humbly acknowledge that only God sees the whole picture.

Your View of Yourself and Others

All of us have a carefully scripted version of ourselves that we allow others to see. We create a mask. We refine it over the years. Physiatrists will tell you it is a natural self-defense mechanism. The mask attempts to protect our true selves from the attack of others. Sub-consciously we learn from an early age that people can be cruel and so we try to protect ourselves. But as Christians, should this be the way we live our lives?

1 John 1:7:

But if we walk in the light as He is in the light, we have fellowship with one another, and the blood of Jesus Christ His Son cleanses us from all sin.

The self-defense mechanism causes us not to be totally open and honest. This damages relationships. Especially close relationships. To be righteous, to be right with God requires the ability to be completely open and honest concerning yourself before God and others.

Micah 1:2:

Hear, all you peoples!
Listen, O earth, and all that is in it!
Let the Lord GOD be a witness against you,
The Lord from His holy temple.

Give to God and others the right to expose and to point out flaws in your life. Let God 'be a witness against you'. As you do, as you allow God and others in, only then will you appropriate the power of the blood of Jesus to heal, to cleanse and to transform.

You will find that exposing your sins and faults does not separate you from God and others, revealing sin actually brings you closer. Don't allow fear to rob you of the freedom found in standing before God and others as your true self.

If not for yourself, walk openly and honestly for the sake of those around you. They need to see the child of God inside. Your true self is accepted and loved before God. Allow God to show you just how much. Allow Him to shower you with His love and acceptance.

By faith, accept and feel His love to the core of your being.

Once you have experienced true love and acceptance from God, you will then be able to show that same love and acceptance towards others. Let me say it more strongly. If you have not received God's unconditional love and acceptance in a meaningful way, you will not have it in you to show the same love to others. But if you have experienced His love, that experience can and will empower you to model unconditional love and acceptance to everyone around you. You will model a freedom from sin that those around you will naturally notice. They will see the freedom and healing found in openness and honesty that they themselves are longing for.

Let me repeat. Your true self is loved and accepted before God. Let this truth sink deep within you. This revelation will empower you to be open and honest towards God and others.

Hebrews 4:13:

And there is no creature hidden from His sight, but all things are naked and open to the eyes of Him to whom we must give account.

As I am writing this, I know that this is a hard teaching. I live and work in the real world. I've had work colleges who I considered friends stab me in the back in front of superiors just to make themselves look better. This doesn't change the fact that the key to having an overcoming life is having no secrets in your life. When you hide secrets you provide a place for Satan to torment you. If admitting you make mistakes costs you your next promotion, maybe that's a good thing. If that other position requires a person to be perfect, then it may not be the best job for you.

The issue of self-protection really boils down to the issue of trust. Do I really believe that God wants the very best for me? Also, exactly what does a glorious, overcoming life really look like? Since we're all different, this answer is different for each of us, but chasing after what the world believes to be important will not get you there.

1 John 3:1-3:

Behold what manner of love the Father has bestowed on us, that we should be called children of God! Therefore the world does not know us, because it did not know Him. ² Beloved, now we are children of God; and it has not yet been revealed what we shall be, but we know that when He is revealed, we shall be like Him, for we shall see Him as He is. ³ And everyone who has this hope in Him purifies himself, just as He is pure.

Your view of yourself needs to be changed. You are a child of God! The unsaved world cannot see this because they don't know Jesus. '*Beloved, now we are children of God*'. It has not yet been revealed to the unbelieving world the person you truly are. But, when Jesus returns you shall be like Him. The key to experiencing the reality of being God's child is to, by faith, seeing yourself as God sees you. Believe the Bible. Believe you are right now a child of God. And then by faith act accordingly.

Learn to walk by faith not by fear.

Your View of the Past

The next view of reality that needs to be changed is your view of your past. You may say that a person cannot change the past. But, you definitely can and need to change your memory of your past. Why? Your memories are actually your interpretations of your past. Even more, your interpretations were formed in your past as well. They are how your past-self interpreted your past event.

This is critically important with childhood memories. Without the healing of the Lord, those past events will continue to be interpreted from the viewpoint of a child.

A common tool in prayer counseling is allowing God to change interpretations of childhood events. This is a critical process for inner healing. You subconsciously still interpret childhood trauma as a child. As a now more-mature Christian that has the understanding that God has always been with you, you need to return to childhood events by way of your imagination and see past events through the eyes of the Lord.

Allow God to give you the mind of Christ concerning past events.

1 Corinthians 2:16:

For "who has known the mind of the Lord that he may instruct Him?" But we have the mind of Christ.

This doesn't mean fooling yourself into believing a bad thing is now good. That's delusion. It means putting events into God's perspective. Most importantly, you need to allow God to comfort and to heal the still hurting child within. Only after healing will you be able to emotionally move past a traumatic event. This last point is simple but very important. Unhealed wounds fester. Don't keep wounds secret. As wounds are brought to the light they can be completely healed.

1 John 2:8:

But if we walk in the light as He is in the light, we have fellowship with one another, and the blood of Jesus Christ His Son cleanses us from all sin.

Live in the light as He is in the light. As you do, Satan will be unable to torment you, because hidden things, things kept in the shadows invite demonic attack upon your mind.

Allowing others to see your wounded soul is scary. You may believe that it makes you vulnerable and open to new attach, but if you do so at the prompting of the Lord, you will find that He is your light and your shield. You will learn to trust in God for your protection. The exhausting task of always keeping your guard up will be replaced by the freedom of trusting in God.

Your View of your Future

The last view of reality that needs to be changed is your view of the future. This includes your view of the workings of God in your present life. As a Christian, much of your glorious future can be experienced now. Heaven is not something confined to your future. Heaven is something you can experience right now.

Yes, right now we are living in a fallen, corrupt world, but the good news is we right now have dual citizenship. We right now can live in two places: earth and heaven. This ability is an incredible gift which most Christians either ignore or are ignorant of. As a result of this ignorance, many suffer through this earthly life without the benefit of daily receiving a heavenly perspective.

Your view of the future needs to expand to include a view of Zion, the New Jerusalem. Since Zion is a mountain (and we're still talking about walking through valleys), we'll postpone the topic of Zion until the end of the book. Before we get to the topic of mountains and the lessons to be learned on each, we need to touch on the topic of the role of the Holy Spirit.

When walking through valleys or across mountain tops, your companion along the way is the Holy Spirit.

Holy Spirit

Psalm 23:4:

Yea, though I walk through the valley of the shadow of death, I will fear no evil; For You are with me; Your rod and Your staff, they comfort me.

You are not meant to walk through valleys alone. If you allow Him, Holy Spirit will be your comforter and guide. He carries a rod to correct you and a staff to pull you back from danger.

Philippians 4:11:13:

I have learned in whatever state I am, to be content: 12 I know how to be abased, and I know how to abound. Everywhere and in all things I have learned both to be full and to be hungry, both to abound and to suffer need. ¹³ I can do all things through Christ who strengthens me.

Holy Spirit descended upon Jesus at His baptism by the hand of John the Baptist. John was what is known as a 'seer prophet'. He could see clearly into the spiritual realm. I believe he had seen the Holy Spirit come to rest upon people before.

John not only had heard the stories of the Holy Spirit coming upon people like David, Samson, Saul and Elijah, but he had seen the Holy Spirit first-hand move upon ordinary people during his ministry. People were turning to God en masse on account of John's ministry. Lives were being dramatically changed. This was obviously the work of the Holy Spirit.

Yet, John was looking for the One upon whom the Holy Spirit would descend and remain.

John 1:32:34:

And John bore witness, saying, "I saw the Spirit descending from heaven like a dove, and He remained upon Him. I did not know Him, but He who sent me to baptize with water said to me, 'Upon whom you see the Spirit descending, and remaining on Him, this is He who baptizes with the Holy Spirit.' And I have seen and testified that this is the Son of God."

It is no small feat to keep a dove on your shoulder for any period of time. But, to have it remain there for your entire life, that is a goal that is only obtainable by God working mightily in the person.

The good news is that the Holy Spirit wants to be ever present in the life of a believer. Holy Spirit is drawn to the Jesus in you. It takes you going against your new nature to temporarily have Holy Spirit lift His feet from your shoulder. But then, once you've regained your senses, once you've come back to your new (true) self, Holy Spirit quickly comes once again upon you.

Micah 6:8:

He has shown you, O man, what is good;
And what does the LORD require of you
But to do justly,
To love mercy,
And to walk humbly with your God?

I love the above verse in Micah. Notice it is written, not as a statement but as a question.

Has He shown you?

If He has, the implication then is; what are you waiting for!?

If He hasn't, then you need to seek the Lord. You need to seek His face.

This is the generation of those who shall ascend the hill of the Lord! They are receiving the blessing from the Lord; righteousness and salvation! Seek Him! Seek His face and the Holy Spirit will be ever present guiding you on your journey through the hills and valleys of the Lord.

> *The Spirit of God in the process of sanctification will strip me until I am nothing but "myself," that is the place of death. Am I willing to be "myself," and nothing more – no friends, no father, no brother, no self-interest – simply ready for death? That is the condition of sanctification. No wonder Jesus said: "I came not to send peace, but a sword."*

> Oswald Chambers
> *My Utmost for His Highest*
> *Barbour Publishing*

Single-mindedness

We make life too complicated for our own good. Life is meant to be simple. Jesus tells us *"seek first the kingdom of God and His righteousness, and all these things shall be added to you."* (Matthew 6:33) The needed quality in your life is single mindedness. The Bible is replete with warnings about being double minded. (James 1:8)

Matthew 6:22-24:

The lamp of the body is the eye. If therefore your eye is good, your whole body will be full of light. 23 But if your eye is bad, your whole body will be full of darkness. If

*therefore the light that is in you is darkness, how
great is that darkness!*

24 *"No one can serve two masters; for either he will hate
the one and love the other, or else he will be loyal to the
one and despise the other. You cannot serve God and
mammon.*

The key to walking through valleys is keeping our eyes on
Jesus. As you learn to set aside the urgent and replace it
with the important, you are allowing yourself to be
transformed by the Lord.

2 Corinthians 3:18:

*But we all, with unveiled face, beholding as in a mirror the
glory of the Lord, are being transformed into the same
image from glory to glory, just as by the Spirit of the Lord.*

Jesus set His face towards Jerusalem. At some point you
need to esteem/seek above all else the love of God. You
need to go beyond your need for the love and acceptance
of man. There's real freedom when you do. You've been
made for this one purpose.

The Larger Catechism of the Westminster Confession got
it right when it states that the 'chief and highest end of
man' is to glorify God and fully to enjoy Him forever.

Matthew 10:37:

He who loves father or mother more than Me is not worthy of Me. And he who loves son or daughter more than Me is not worthy of Me.

Husbands are instructed to leave father and mother and to cling unto their spouse. This is symbolic of the greater goal of leaving behind the world system and seeking only the Kingdom of God. We are called to be in the world but not of it. We are called to be salt and light in a dull and dark place. You do this by being a 'called out', separated, holy person.

Most are not called to a single life, but all are called to be routinely alone.

You need to come to know a level of intimacy and fellowship with the Holy Spirit that is simply impossible (in this life) to achieve with other people. It is the felt need (if only at first at a sub-conscience level) for such personnel intimacy that is drawing you to the Lord.

You were not created to have only shallow relationships. You were created for close intimate relationships, especially with God. I cherish the relationships in my life. They are gifts from God. But, I hold them loosely as the delicate flowers they are. To expect them to achieve the deep level of intimacy that only the Holy Spirit can achieve will surely crush them. This not to blame yourself, your friends or others, it's simply not obtainable in a human relationship here on earth. Even with the perfect friend or partner, you both will be limited by the imperfect communication avenues available physically.

Psalm 42:7:

Deep calls unto deep at the noise of Your waterfalls;
All Your waves and billows have gone over me.

You are a spiritual being. Your spirit and the Holy Spirit call out to each other!

Song of Solomon 2:10:

My beloved spoke, and said to me:
"Rise up, my love, my fair one,
And come away.

Heed the Holy Spirit's call. Then the other things in your life will fall into correct order. As a loving Father, God will provide the other things. And they will be in correct portions and timings.

Summary

Allow Holy Spirit, the comforter to comfort you, to sooth the bumps and bruises that you get in the world. Don't seek the comfort that comes from the world. The world tries to mask pain. The Holy Spirit heals pain.

John 14:27:

Peace I leave with you, My peace I give to you; not as the world gives do I give to you. Let not your heart be troubled, neither let it be afraid.

To experience God's holy mountains, you must first learn the way of repentance in the valleys. You must understand what true repentance is. It is a daily submitting of yourself to God for the purpose of allowing Him to transform you into the image of His Son. You need to lay aside what worldly experience has taught you and allow God to show you a radically different way to live. If you allow Him, He will radically change your views of reality.

Enough about valleys, let's talk about mountains!

Mountains

The mountains of Israel represent the promises of God to Israel and to the church. In Ezekiel chapter 36, there is a prophecy that states that the mountains will "shoot forth branches," and "yield fruit" to God's people. I believe that one such intended fruit is that God's people will learn the lessons of intimacy as they learn the object lessons found on the mountains of Israel. The prophecy in Ezekiel includes the promise that ...

Ezekiel 36:26-27:

I will give you a new heart and put a new spirit within you; I will take the heart of stone out of your flesh and give you a heart of flesh. [27] I will put My Spirit within you and cause you to walk in My statutes, and you will keep My judgments and do them.

John's Recorded Miracles

The Lord has shown me that the path to hearing and abiding with God on a daily basis is not a journey up one mountain but regularly visiting several. Each mountain represents a lesson to be learned in your journey in the things of God. God will call you to spend extended times in contemplative prayer on each mountain as He works out things in your life by revealing things about Himself.

In the New Testament, the same lessons can be found in the seven miracles recorded in the Gospel of John. In the following pages, specific mountains of Israel will be followed by corresponding miracles from John's Gospel.

John states the follow reason for including these particular miracles in his gospel, he states:

John 20:30-31:

And truly Jesus did many other signs in the presence of His disciples, which are not written in this book; [31] but these are written that you may believe that Jesus is the Christ, the Son of God, and that believing you may have life in His name.

And so, the purpose of the lessons on the mountains and the purpose of the recorded miracles are the same. Namely, to point people to Jesus, to teach people how to have life in His name.

Having abundant life in His name is the goal of the Christian life. Living an abundant overcoming life is the purpose behind spending time in the spirit atop the mountains of God contemplating the lessons of the seven miracles recorded by John.

Mount Ararat – Peace and Rest

Genesis 8:4:

Then the ark rested in the seventh month, the seventeenth day of the month, on the mountains of Ararat.

A visit to Mount Ararat in the spirit is a visit to a place of peace and rest. I find it interesting that upon arrival to Ararat, Noah, a person who worked incredibly hard most of his adult life on building the ark, immediately planted a vineyard. Yes. He over did it with drinking the wine, but I believe that happened partly because he was overwhelmed at the spirit of peace and rest that occupies Ararat.

Isaiah 11:6-9:

The wolf also shall dwell with the lamb,
The leopard shall lie down with the young goat,
The calf and the young lion and the fatling together;
And a little child shall lead them.
7 The cow and the bear shall graze;
Their young ones shall lie down together;
And the lion shall eat straw like the ox.
8 The nursing child shall play by the cobra's hole,
And the weaned child shall put his hand in the viper's den.
9 They shall not hurt nor destroy in all My holy mountain,
For the earth shall be full of the knowledge of the LORD
As the waters cover the sea.

In the above passage, I believe that Isaiah is describing a visit to Ararat. When you visit Ararat in the spirit, you see the animals lying down together. Peace and calm surrounds everything.

This is the first of the spiritual mountains all Christians must visit. It teaches the first lesson in hearing and abiding with God: Peace and Rest. When you are anxious and troubled in your spirit, God is calling you to visit Mount Ararat. Let it calm your spirit. Feel the peace.

Hearing God starts with a peaceful calm mind and a restful soul. You need to learn to go to Ararat in the spirit of your mind. You need to routinely spend time in this incredible place of peace and rest.

You need to stay in the place of peace and rest in God, specifically in the person of the Holy Spirit. This may seem obvious, but it is a heard lesson for many to learn. You must practice the discipline of letting go and being at peace.

Letting go is hard. It requires absolute trust in another person. Noah and his family in the ark trusted that God was going to take care of them and that the flood was going to subside. As the waves crash around you in your life, how completely are you going to trust in God to calm the storm?

To visit Mount Ararat means to learn the lesson Jesus taught by turning water into wine. By turning water into wine, Jesus emphasizes the need for Holy Spirit joy in a person's life. This life is a gift. It is meant to be enjoyed. Your life is meant to be filled with overflowing joy.

Changing Water into Wine
John 2:1-11:

On the third day there was a wedding in Cana of Galilee, and the mother of Jesus was there. ² Now both Jesus and His disciples were invited to the wedding. ³ And when they ran out of wine, the mother of Jesus said to Him, "They have no wine."

⁴ Jesus said to her, "Woman, what does your concern have to do with Me? My hour has not yet come."

⁵ His mother said to the servants, "Whatever He says to you, do it."

⁶ Now there were set there six water pots of stone, according to the manner of purification of the Jews, containing twenty or thirty gallons apiece. ⁷ Jesus said to them, "Fill the water pots with water." And they filled them up to the brim. ⁸ And He said to them, "Draw some out now, and take it to the master of the feast." And they took it. ⁹ When the master of the feast had tasted the water that was made wine, and did not know where it came from (but the servants who had drawn the water knew), the master of the feast called the bridegroom. ¹⁰ And he said to him, "Every man at the beginning sets out the good wine, and when the guests have well drunk, then the inferior. You have kept the good wine until now!"

¹¹ This beginning of signs Jesus did in Cana of Galilee, and manifested His glory; and His disciples believed in Him.

The world has run out of wine. Pause and feel the truth in that statement. As a Christian, the wine you are looking for cannot be found in the world. Wine is symbolic of happiness and joy. Biblically, wine is symbolic of the joy of the Holy Spirit. Every day you need the joy of the Holy Spirit. This is not optional. If you are living your life without joy, spend time each day with Jesus contemplating the Marriage in Cana of Galilee.

Both Jesus and His disciples were invited to the wedding. That invitation still stands.

You are one of Jesus' disciples. Return in the spirit once again to spend time with Jesus at the Marriage in Cana of Galilee.

Jesus told His mother, *"My hour has not yet come."* That is no longer true. Jesus' hour of suffering and dying, His hour of being raised and glorified did indeed come. He has been glorified. He now sits on His throne in heaven. He is now inviting you to join the celebration!

Mary's advice to the servants now applies to you. *"Whatever He says to you, do it."* His direction will lead you to the celebration. Follow what He is speaking to you. For each person His direction will be different. Pause and listen to the voice of the Lord on a daily basis. He will guide you and give you direction for your day.

"Now there were set there six water pots of stone ..." Six is the number of man. People try lots of hard things to try to purify or redeem the things of this world and themselves.

Jesus' way of purifying starts with repentance and then filling you to the brim with the joy of the Holy Spirit. Then, once He has filled you, He will draw you out. He will use you to show the world His wine. His joyous filling is better than anything the world has to offer. He will turn ordinary things into supernatural things. He will turn water into wine.

The wine of the Lord gets better and better with age.

This is the beginning. This is the first lesson to start our tour of the high places of God. Believe in the Lord. Thirst for the infilling of the Holy Spirit in your life. This will manifest His glory in your life. The Lord wants you to live a joyous abundant life.

Abundant Life
John 10:10:

The thief does not come except to steal, and to kill, and to destroy. I have come that they may have life, and that they may have it more abundantly.

Jesus' stated reason for His ministry is for you to have an abundant life.

What does such a life look like? A life where you are continually filled to the brim with the joy of the Holy Spirit? Jesus died so that you would have an abundant life full of joy and the supernatural! That is the life that Jesus died to give you!

Does such a life look a little strange? It may look odd in the world's eyes, but NOT in God's eyes. Picture in your mind what your supernatural life would look like. Picture a life where supernatural healing and provision are your expected norm. Meditate on it. Allow God to show you yourself walking out such a life. Allow yourself to dream about such a supernatural life. Then as God prompts you, in faith, step into that life. Start by praying for those around you. Start by expecting miracles to occur around you. Start by looking for what God is doing around you.

Pray that God opens your eyes! Pray and expect the supernatural to happen in your life.

Don't be ashamed to be the only truly drunk person in the room, drunk, of course, on the joy of the Holy Spirit. Be drunk by being filled with God!

Picture yourself at the wedding feast table as an honored guest. You are at the head table with Jesus. What is Jesus doing? How is He acting? Is He sad or happy? Is He having a good time? Of course, He is! Are you accepted at the wedding? Are people glad you are there as well? Of course, they are! Linger at the party. Let Jesus show you around the marvelous wedding celebration He longs to show you!

What is the value of using your imagination in this way? Is there value in such an exercise/experience?

How different will your day/morning be after you leave the wedding party? Hopefully you stay a little intoxicated in the gladness and joy of the wine for the rest of your day!

Mount Moriah – Sacrifice and Worship
Genesis 22:2:

Now it came to pass after these things that God tested Abraham, and said to him, "Abraham!" And he said, "Here I am." ² Then He said, "Take now your son, your only son Isaac, whom you love, and go to the land of Moriah, and offer him there as a burnt offering on one of the mountains of which I shall tell you."

The capacity to sacrifice joyfully comes from the Lord. It is imparted and is part of the spirit of the Lord Jesus Christ in your life. It is enabled as He gives you spiritual vision of your future. Growing in faith and trust in God for that future are required. You need to learn to let go and trust.

Hebrews 12:1-2:

Therefore we also, since we are surrounded by so great a cloud of witnesses, let us lay aside every weight, and the sin which so easily ensnares us, and let us run with endurance the race that is set before us, ² looking unto

Jesus, the author and finisher of our faith, who for the joy that was set before Him endured the cross, despising the shame, and has sat down at the right hand of the throne of God.

Where are you sitting in heaven? You're with Jesus. You're sitting with Jesus at the right hand of the throne. You are accepted in the throne room of God. God is for you, not against you. You are His child. Learn to view your life through the eyes of the Lord and so be a person of praise and worship. Learn to have God's vision of your future and so let go of those things in your life that are not God's best.

Learn to spend time in the spirit on Mount Moriah. Mount Moriah is the place where you lay down things. Things you were never meant to carry in the first place. Lay down the cares and worries of this life. Lay them down and learn to worship the Lord. Take His yoke upon you and learn of the Lord. His yoke is easy and His burden is light. (Matthew 11:28)

To be a person who hears the voice of God, you must to learn to be a person of sacrifice and worship. You must learn to turn away from the temporary things of this world and so learn the joy of taking comfort in only the eternal things of God.

Hebrews 11:24-27:

By faith Moses, when he became of age, refused to be called the son of Pharaoh's daughter, [25] choosing rather to suffer affliction with the people of God than to enjoy the passing pleasures of sin, 26 esteeming the reproach of Christ greater riches than the treasures in Egypt; for he looked to the reward.

27 By faith he forsook Egypt, not fearing the wrath of the king; for he endured as seeing Him who is invisible.

Moses chose sacrifice. He esteemed the reproach of having Christ (the anointing of God on his life), greater riches than anything the world had to offer. He did this by *"seeing Him who is invisible"*.

Here are two examples of what happens upon Mount Moriah …

King David and Mount Moriah

Mount Moriah is the location of the threshing floor that King David bought from Araunah the Jebusite. (2 Samuel 24:18) It was when David was given three choices of retribution for his sin: 1. Seven years of famine, 2. Three months fleeing from your enemies or 3. Three days' plague in the land. David chose to *"fall into the hand of the LORD, for His mercies are great; but do not let me fall into the hand of man"*. (2 Samuel 24:14) David chose option three.

2 Samuel 24:15-17:

So the LORD sent a plague upon Israel from the morning till the appointed time. From Dan to Beersheba seventy thousand men of the people died. ¹⁶ *And when the angel stretched out His hand over Jerusalem to destroy it, the LORD relented from the destruction, and said to the angel who was destroying the people, "It is enough; now restrain your hand." And the angel of the LORD was by the threshing floor of Araunah the Jebusite.*

¹⁷ *Then David spoke to the LORD when he saw the angel who was striking the people, and said, "Surely I have sinned, and I have done wickedly; but these sheep, what have they done? Let Your hand, I pray, be against me and against my father's house."*

Seeing the angel and hearing the voice of God caused David to purchase the threshing floor. Afterwards, *David built there an altar to the LORD, and offered burnt offerings and peace offerings. So the LORD heeded the prayers for the land, and the plague was withdrawn from Israel.* (2 Samuel 24:25)

Mount Moriah is a place of seeing angels and hearing the voice of God. Believe me, this will definitely cause you to sacrifice everything and worship the Lord!

Abraham and Mount Moriah

Mount Moriah is the location where Abraham offered his son Isaac to the Lord. Abraham went to Mount Moriah at the prompting of the Lord.

Genesis 22:1-2:

Now it came to pass after these things that God tested Abraham, and said to him, "Abraham!" And he said, "Here I am." ² Then He said, "Take now your son, your only son Isaac, whom you love, and go to the land of Moriah, and offer him there as a burnt offering on one of the mountains of which I shall tell you."

In the Bible, Abraham is continually held up as a person to emulate. I believe this is because of his ability to see his promised future. Throughout his life Abraham clung to the promise of God that his descendants would be as many as the stars in the sky (Genesis 15:5).

Mount Moriah is a place of seeing your promised future.

Allow God to show you His promises for you. Allow God to give you a vision for your future that looks beyond small beginnings, that looks beyond past mistakes. And with that vision in mind, lay down everything you once relied upon Mount Moriah. Only then will you have the clarity of vision to see God's provision and God's way forward. And then, step out in faith worshipping God for what He is about to do!

Healing the Nobleman's Son
John 4:46-54:

So Jesus came again to Cana of Galilee where He had made the water wine. And there was a certain nobleman whose son was sick at Capernaum. ⁴⁷ When he heard that Jesus had come out of Judea into Galilee, he went to Him and implored Him to come down and heal his son, for he was at the point of death. ⁴⁸ Then Jesus said to him, "Unless you people see signs and wonders, you will by no means believe."

⁴⁹ The nobleman said to Him, "Sir, come down before my child dies!"

⁵⁰ Jesus said to him, "Go your way; your son lives." So the man believed the word that Jesus spoke to him, and he went his way. ⁵¹ And as he was now going down, his servants met him and told him, saying, "Your son lives!"

⁵² Then he inquired of them the hour when he got better. And they said to him, "Yesterday at the seventh hour the fever left him." ⁵³ So the father knew that it was at the same hour in which Jesus said to him, "Your son lives." And he himself believed, and his whole household.

⁵⁴ This again is the second sign Jesus did when He had come out of Judea into Galilee.

In the healing of the nobleman's son we have the second lesson needed to understand about life in the spirit. Namely, life in the spirit is outside the restrictions of time and distance. In the spirit you can be in different places at the same time. You can revisit the past. You can see the future. You are not restricted by time or location.

In the spirit, God will remind you of past trauma. If He does, take the past hurt to Mount Moriah and there lay down the burden you've been carrying. It's time to let it go! Redeem the time that has been lost! Let God give you a vision of a future life freed from the pain of the past. Then in faith begin to live that life.

In the spirit, perhaps God will lay it on your heart to pray for someone who is far away. In response we need to learn to, by faith, see ourselves next to that person praying and interceding. Distance is not an issue. Your prayers can be just as effective from where you are as if you were physically with them.

Not only are we not restricted by distance, but we are also not restricted by time. Most Christians try to make it a point to pray for those who are sick or who are going through a hospital procedure. We try to remember to pray during the time of their sickness or procedure. That's great but we can pray right now for healing and protection for a day in the future. 'Give us this day our daily bread' is actually such a prayer.

We also can return in the spirit to event/times in our past to allow God to heal ourselves, to heal relationships and to break past curses or pronouncements spoken against us or those we love.

Jesus is called the Lamb slain from the foundation of the world. (Revelation 13:8) He is the alpha and the omega, the beginning and the end. (Revelation 1:8) He is right now the past and the future. Why are all these things true? It is because He is and we are spiritual beings, and thus we are not bound by time or distance.

John 4:49-51:

The nobleman said to Him, "Sir, come down before my child dies!"

50 Jesus said to him, "Go your way; your son lives." So the man believed the word that Jesus spoke to him, and he went his way. 51 And as he was now going down, his servants met him and told *him,* saying, "Your son lives!"

The lesson the nobleman teaches us is that he came to believe Jesus could heal at a distance just by a spoken word. This was not true before his encounter with Jesus. *"Sir, come down before my child dies!"* (John 4:49) This was the nobleman's initial level of faith. He believed that healers needed to be physically touching those who would be healed. Jesus' response was: *"Go your way; your son lives."* (John 4:50) How did Jesus know that it was the nobleman's son? The nobleman had simply said 'child'.

When you read verses 49 and 50, pause between them. The nobleman was clearly humbly longing for a touch from Jesus. I don't believe Jesus' answer came quickly or was dismissive. I believe that Jesus' response was very deliberant and was delivered in such a tone that the man's understanding of God was forever changed. *"Go your way; your son lives."*

So the man believed the word that Jesus spoke to him, and he went his way.

If our first spiritual lesson while experiencing God's holy mountains is that we need to be drunk in the wine of the Holy Spirit, our second lesson is to stop at the promptings of the Holy Spirit and without regard to time or distance, intercede and expect healing and resurrection to occur.

If our first lesson is that we need a place of peace and rest to center ourselves on God, our second lesson is we need to then follow the Holy Spirit throughout the day as He shows us what God is doing in the spirit.

Following the Holy Spirit throughout the day requires sacrifice. It requires us to allow God to interrupt our plans, to supplant our agenda with His own. Like David we must learn to allow God to be in control. Like Abraham we must learn to view today in how it plays into our future.

The reward in resting and trusting in a God is you become a person who worships God for all He has done, for all He is doing and for all He has yet to do.

The Mount of Beatitudes – Spiritual Eyesight

Matthew 5:1-3:

And seeing the multitudes, He went up on a mountain, and when He was seated His disciples came to Him. ²Then He opened His mouth and taught them, saying: ³"Blessed are the poor in spirit, For theirs is the kingdom of heaven.

It is believed that the location of the Sermon on the Mount is a slope in the vicinity of Capernaum. The sermon is considered the greatest ever delivered by Jesus Himself.

To read the Sermon on the Mount as goals to be achieved is to miss the point. To read the sermon as moral guidance to follow makes Jesus just another philosopher or moral teacher. No. The attributes mentioned in the sermon: to be poor in spirit, to be meek, to be merciful, to be pure in heart, to be peacemakers are not the goals of Christianity (as if someone could achieve any of them by their own self-effort). They are the changes that happen to a person as they spend time in the spirit with the Lord.

As you spend time in the spirit with the Lord, Jesus imparts these virtues. They are not attained by following religious rituals. Spending time with the Lord is the only path to attainment. This is why intimacy is the only path we are called to follow. To His disciples, Jesus commanded just one thing: *"come and follow me"*. (Matthew 19:21)

Some personal change will be gradual. You may not even notice it is occurring.

The lesson to learn on The Mount of Beatitudes is clear. Jesus wants us to see the fallacy found in religious ritual and dogma. Christianity is about living a bought and paid for transformed life. It's about discovering the new person that we are in Christ. We've been changed into His image. We're to be salt and light to the world.

As salt and light we will defeat the satanic lies associated with unbelief and superstition. How will we do that? We overcome Satan by the blood of the Lamb and by the word of our testimony!

Revelation 12:10-11:

Then I heard a loud voice saying in heaven, "Now salvation, and strength, and the kingdom of our God, and the power of His Christ have come, for the accuser of our brethren, who accused them before our God day and night, has been cast down. 11 And they overcame him by the blood of the Lamb and by the word of their testimony, and they did not love their lives to the death.

The blood of Jesus Christ bought us. We've been redeemed. As now part of His body, we are infused with His blood. We are bone of His bone and flesh of His flesh. (Genesis 2:23) We are washed. The blood of Jesus Christ has cleansed. We are healed. We are restored.

Then, our testimony is not just the stories we tell (no matter how glorious), but also our minute-by-minute holy, redeemed, overcoming life. Our testimony is that we approach each day from a heavenly perspective. Going into every situation, our viewpoint and expectation is completely different than those who do not know nor follow the Lamb wherever He goes. (Revelation 14:4)

Healing at the Pool of Bethesda
John 5:1-8:

After this there was a feast of the Jews, and Jesus went up to Jerusalem. ² Now there is in Jerusalem by the Sheep Gate a pool, which is called in Hebrew, Bethesda^j having five porches. ³ In these lay a great multitude of sick people, blind, lame, paralyzed, waiting for the moving of the water. ⁴ For an angel went down at a certain time into the pool and stirred up the water; then whoever stepped in first, after the stirring of the water, was made well of whatever disease he had ⁵ Now a certain man was there who had an infirmity thirty-eight years. ⁶ When Jesus saw him lying there, and knew that he already had been in that condition a long time, He said to him, "Do you want to be made well?"

⁷ The sick man answered Him, "Sir, I have no man to put me into the pool when the water is stirred up; but while I am coming, another steps down before me."

8 Jesus said to him, "Rise, take up your bed and walk." 9 And immediately the man was made well, took up his bed, and walked.

The third spiritual lesson while experiencing God's holy hills comes from Jesus' teaching after He heals the man at the pool of Bethesda. The spiritual lesson is this. As a Child of God, developing your spiritual eyes is critical. The man was supernaturally healed in no small part because Jesus could clearly see the spiritual condition behind the physical condition. Let me highlight two points as backdrop to the story:

1. The man had been lying there a long time. His condition had become a part of him for He saw himself as a sick person. He believed Satan's lie about himself.

2. He had bought into a cultural superstition. He believed in the power of angels and so was not being healed.

Aside ...

> Some believe such superstitions are at most harmless. Yet, the Bible is clear in that we should not worship angels (or any other spirit). We worship Jesus alone.
>
> John 5:17-18:
>
> *Jesus answered them, "My Father has been working until now, and I have been working."*

18 Therefore the Jews sought all the more to kill Him, because He not only broke the Sabbath, but also said that God was His Father, making Himself equal with God.

We worship Jesus alone because Jesus alone is God. Jesus repeatedly called God his father. In this he equated Himself with God. This is the issue that most offended His Jewish audience.

The spiritual lesson which Jesus demonstrated at the Pool of Bethesda is critical for all children of God. By it Jesus emphasizes the criticalness of developing spiritual eyesight.

John 5:19-20:

Then Jesus answered and said to them, "Most assuredly, I say to you, the Son can do nothing of Himself, <u>but what He sees the Father do</u>; for whatever He does, the Son also does in like manner. 20 For the Father loves the Son, and shows Him all things that He Himself does; and He will show Him greater works than these, that you may marvel. (My underline)

As a Child of God, on a daily basis you need to <u>see</u> what Father God is doing so that you can follow His lead. The good news is Father God loves to show you what He is doing. The Holy Spirit is the enabler of your spiritual eyesight.

Why is spiritual eyesight so critical?

Without spiritual eyesight, we are prone to fall into the same lies found in the man at the Pool of Bethesda.

I believe the man at the Pool of Bethesda was blinded by the two main lies that God will have His true sons defeat in the days ahead: The lie that some believe that they are made sick by God and can never be made whole and the lie that some believe that they should fear things of the spirit.

As a Son of God, you are meant to rule and reign. You are not to see yourself as weak or sick. Each of us has direct access to the throne room of God to find healing and strength to help in time of need. (Hebrews 4:16)

The two battles to be fought are unbelief (belief in a lie) and superstition (worship of things other than Jesus). Here the Lord presents us with the two main tasks of the true Sons of God. By speaking forth what we have seen and heard from Father God, by living a life of holiness and power we are to defeat the two enemies of the Lord: unbelief and superstition.

Mount Nebo – Vision and Death
Deuteronomy 32:52:

Then the LORD spoke to Moses that very same day, saying:
49 "Go up this mountain of the Abarim, Mount Nebo, which

is in the land of Moab, across from Jericho; view the land of Canaan, which I give to the children of Israel as a possession; 50 and die on the mountain which you ascend, and be gathered to your people, just as Aaron your brother died on Mount Hor and was gathered to his people; 51 because you trespassed against Me among the children of Israel at the waters of Meribah Kadesh, in the Wilderness of Zin, because you did not hallow Me in the midst of the children of Israel. 52 Yet you shall see the land before you, though you shall not go there, into the land which I am giving to the children of Israel."

The last event in the life of Moses provides a great object lesson for all generations; namely, the link between vision and death. Mount Nebo is the location where God showed Moses the Promised Land. It is also where Moses died. Afterwards, the Lord Himself carried the body of Moses down to a valley (opposite Beth Peor) and buried him. The next time we see Moses in the Bible is on the Mount of Transfiguration (probably Mount Tabor) with Jesus and Elijah. (Mark 9:2-4)

In the spirit, vision and death are always linked. This might sound scary when in fact it is meant to be joyous. This is because to truly have a vision for the best, the mediocre must die. To truly have a vision for the eternal, the temporary must die.

2 Corinthians 2:9:

Yes, we had the sentence of death in ourselves, that we should not trust in ourselves but in God who raises the dead.

It is a good thing to have the *'sentence of death'*. It means that God is working in your life to change you for the good. He is working to kill the temporal for the sake of the eternal. God will shake all things so that only those things that cannot be shaken will remain (Hebrews 12:27)

A problem occurs when we lose sight of the vision and yet the process of death in our lives is still continuing. Without vision the people perish. (Proverbs 29:18)

We start out in life with such grand hopes and dreams. The process of maturity is a process of death as we see most of our initial dreams die. But, by the grace of God, our initial shallow, self-centered dreams get replaced with much deeper, eternal dreams.

A quick wit is replaced with quiet wisdom. A sharp tongue is replaced with forgiveness and grace.

Some initial dreams do come true. The arrival at many of these destinations only reveals their true shallow nature. We arrive and ask ourselves: Is this it? Is this what I've worked so hard to achieve?

God taking Moses to Mount Nebo was not a time of sorrow. God was showing Moses that his descendants would possess the Promised Land. Though He himself would not enter in, he could rest in the peace of knowing that his life's work had not been in vain.

This is what happens once we get past our own selfish dreams. God replaces them with the dreams which last into eternity, which we were created to achieve. Through the new dreams we discover our true selves. And so, self realization comes not from self introspection but by God revelation. (1 John 3:2)

Through new God-inspired dreams we discover not only our true selves, but the true nature of God.

Through allowing God to replace our dreams with His, you allow God to reveal the person you were predestined to be. (Romans 8:29) Through the process of dying to (letting go of) the old dreams and embracing new dreams, self confusion and doubt are gradually replaced. This is not so much a process of change but of discovery. God reveals to you the person that He created.

If you have the subconscious feeling that you were created for more than your current circumstance, you're right. You were created for grandeur. You were created for a God-given purpose.

Ephesians 2:10:

For we are His workmanship, created in Christ Jesus for good works, which God prepared beforehand that we should walk in them.

Spend time in the spirit upon Mount Nebo. Allow God to impart to you His dreams. You will find them to be beyond anything you can image. In them you will come to know the true nature of Father God. (Ephesians 3:20)

Feeding the 5000
John 6:1-14:

After these things Jesus went over the Sea of Galilee, which is the Sea of Tiberias. [2] Then a great multitude followed Him, because they saw His signs which He performed on those who were diseased. [3] And Jesus went up on the mountain, and there He sat with His disciples.

[4] Now the Passover, a feast of the Jews, was near. [5] Then Jesus lifted up His eyes, and seeing a great multitude coming toward Him, He said to Philip, "Where shall we buy bread, that these may eat?" [6] But this He said to test him, for He Himself knew what He would do.

[7] Philip answered Him, "Two hundred denarii worth of bread is not sufficient for them, that every one of them may have a little."

[8] One of His disciples, Andrew, Simon Peter's brother, said to Him, [9] "There is a lad here who has five barley loaves and two small fish, but what are they among so many?"

[10] Then Jesus said, "Make the people sit down." Now there was much grass in the place. So the men sat down, in

number about five thousand. [11] And Jesus took the loaves, and when He had given thanks He distributed them to the disciples, and the disciple] to those sitting down; and likewise of the fish, as much as they wanted. [12] So when they were filled, He said to His disciples, "Gather up the fragments that remain, so that nothing is lost." [13] Therefore they gathered them up, and filled twelve baskets with the fragments of the five barley loaves which were left over by those who had eaten. [14] Then those men, when they had seen the sign that Jesus did, said, "This is truly the Prophet who is to come into the world."

The goal of being a Christian mystic, of spending daily time contemplating heaven and the Lord, is to come to know His true nature. Only by spending time with someone do you truly come to know their heart.

So many Christians spend their lives simply learning about Jesus by reading about Him. That's fine in some ways. You should want to learn all you can about Jesus. But, reading a book about someone and the impartation you receive by spending time with that same person are two totally different things.

Then those men, when they had seen the sign that Jesus did, said, "This is truly the Prophet who is to come into the world." (John 6:14)

In the feeding of the five thousand, the men saw, perhaps for the first time in their lives, a glimpse of the true nature of God. They had been so accustomed to religion they lost sight of God. The true nature of God is the true nature of fatherhood: loving, caring, self-sacrificing, accepting, protector and provider. The message of Jesus is clear. God cares and provides for His children.

John 14:1-2:

Let not your heart be troubled; you believe in God, believe also in Me. ² In My Father's house are many mansions; if it were not so, I would have told you. I go to prepare a place for you.

Matthew 6:31-33:

"Therefore do not worry, saying, 'What shall we eat?' or 'What shall we drink?' or 'What shall we wear?'³² For after all these things the Gentiles seek. For your heavenly Father knows that you need all these things. ³³ But seek first the kingdom of God and His righteousness, and all these things shall be added to you.

Matthew 7:11:

If you then, being evil, know how to give good gifts to your children, how much more will your Father who is in heaven give good things to those who ask Him!

Your Father is in heaven. You need to go to Him and ask for good things! And yet, the vast majority of Christians find the idea of actually standing in the heavenly throne room either impossible or too dangerous to attempt.

Some believe the lie that says that you can't go to heaven right now. Some believe the lie that by somehow traveling down the mystic path that they will be lead astray into doctrinal error.

James 1:5-7:

If any of you lacks wisdom, let him ask of God, who gives to all liberally and without reproach, and it will be given to him. 6 But let him ask in faith, with no doubting, for he who doubts is like a wave of the sea driven and tossed by the wind. 7 For let not that man suppose that he will receive anything from the Lord; 8 he is a double-minded man, unstable in all his ways.

I've written many times about the need in a person's life to stay continually aware of their dual citizenship, of being constantly aware of the fact they are at this moment both here in the physical realm and in heaven in the spiritual realm. This is not the double mindedness spoken of in the Book of James. On the contrary, walking through the day with a heavenly awareness is the key to being a stable, self-assured, joyful person. You'll find yourself being the most stable person in the room! That's because you have a guiding light in your life a constant northern star, a heavenly beacon providing steady direction in every situation. Being heavenly minded gives you God's eternal perspective on what is going on around you at that moment in the natural.

The person who wavers between belief in God and reliance on themselves or on the world is the double mined man. They waver back and forth between two mindsets, between two world views. Is God really in control? Can I really trust in God?

The key to staying single minded is keeping your eyes on God and on His promises. Spend time on Mount Nebo. Allow God to show you how the process of death in your life is actually bringing about the vision He has for you. Remember, without vision the people perish

Mount Sinai – Calling and Separation
Exodus 19:1-3:

In the third month after the children of Israel had gone out of the land of Egypt, on the same day, they came to the Wilderness of Sinai. ² For they had departed from Rephidim, had come tothe Wilderness of Sinai, and camped in the wilderness. So Israel camped there before the mountain. ³ And Moses went up to God, and the LORD called to him from the mountain …

Of the mountains I visit during my contemplation times with the Lord, none is more awe inspiring than Mount Sinai. A mountain that *"burned with fire, and to blackness and darkness and tempest"* that was so terrifying that Moses said, *"I am exceedingly afraid and trembling"*. During such visits the Lord reminds me that we Christians, *"the general assembly and church of the firstborn who are registered in heaven"*, reside in a much more awe inspiring place called Mount Zion, the city of the living God, the heavenly Jerusalem. (Hebrews 12:18-24)

I much prefer lush green of the forest to the stark rouged heights of Sinai. I much prefer the still small voice of God to the thundering voice heard on Mount Sinai. But hear it I must. For if I don't tremble (in a good way) occasionally, I'm not truly encountering Yahweh.

In Old Testament times, for the most part, the word of God came corporately to the children of Israel. They lived by the handed down corporate law of God. While it is still true that God can give corporate direction to a body of believers, it is clear that as Christians we are called to be a law unto ourselves. (Romans 2:14)

Romans 2:28-29:

For he is not a Jew who is one outwardly, nor is circumcision that which is outward in the flesh; [29] but he is a Jew who is one inwardly; and circumcision is that of the heart, in the Spirit, not in the letter; whose praise is not from men but from God.

Before being the location where God gave to Moses the Ten Commandments, Mount Sinai was the location where Moses received his calling to be the deliverer of God's chosen people Israel. It was the location of Moses' burning bush. I call it Moses' burning bush because it was lit for one person.

As Christians we all need Mount Sinai. We all need our own burning bush encounter with God. (Exodus 3:2) This is because we all need the same transformation from God. Before Mount Sinai, Moses was running away from God and his people. At the burning bush, God changed his heart forever. Afterwards, Moses had a burning love for God and for God's people. We all need the same 'baptism of love'.

No matter what our occupation, we're all called to a supernatural love for those around us. By supernatural, I mean a heart of love for everyone, for the rude and for the unkind. Such love is only possible by a supernatural change of heart given by God. God must replace your heart with His own heart. You must acquire God's heart for people.

Do you desire to move in the prophetic? Do you desire to minister and express God's love to others? It begins with God changing your heart. Pray for God to give you supernatural love for people. Then be sensitive to His promptings to pray and to intercede for others. If God fills your heart with love for another person, then they will sense it in every conversation. Without the need to proclaim "thus says the Lord" all your speech will be prophetic. They will sense God in you. You will be a written epistle. (2 Corinthians 3:2)

Walking on Water
John 6:15-21:

Therefore when Jesus perceived that they were about to come and take Him by force to make Him king, He departed again to the mountain by Himself alone.

[16] Now when evening came, His disciples went down to the sea, [17] got into the boat, and went over the sea toward Capernaum. And it was already dark, and Jesus had not come to them. [18] Then the sea arose because a great wind was blowing. [19] So when they had rowed about three or four miles,[b] they saw Jesus walking on the sea and drawing near the boat; and they were afraid. [20] But He said to them, "It is I; do not be afraid." [21] Then they willingly received Him into the boat, and immediately the boat was at the land where they were going.

My walks in heavenly places with Jesus have in large part been a transformation of the mind, a reconnecting of the mind with spiritual truths. I believe such foundational truths need to be established in a person's life before the Lord can move forward. (Hebrews 6:1-3) With that said, when I read/ponder the account of Jesus walking on the water, I'm suddenly stopped in my tracks. The transformation of the mind through reconnecting with heaven is one thing. The manifestation of the supernatural in the natural world is another thing all together.

As I sat with Jesus in contemplation, I asked Him, "I know that everything you did on earth in front of your disciples was an object lesson for us all. Why did you walk on water? What was the lesson?" His answer was immediate and full of peace. The lesson is ... I'm God and you're not. I can walk on water. I can multiply fish and loaves.

His answer brought tremendous peace. There is great comfort in the fact we have a loving Father God who is in control. All attempts of people to control nature are attempts to be gods themselves. The supernatural is available by asking and praying to God, but it is only God who is supernatural. Man is of nature. God is above nature. Signs, wonders and miracles are meant to be proof of God, not the exaltation of man.

This is the lesson of Mount Sinai. This is the lesson of Jesus walking on the water.

This left me with the question then of how do we as Christians fit into God's creation? Are we not spiritual ourselves? Are we not (dare I say) supernatural ourselves?

John 17:16:
They are not of the world, just as I am not of the world.

Hebrews 2:6:8:
What is man that You are mindful of him,
Or the son of man that You take care of him?
7 You have made him a little lower than the angels;
You have crowned him with glory and honor,
And set him over the works of Your hands.
8 You have put all things in subjection under his feet."

God's answer to my question: We're stewards. We take care of God's creation. Here on earth, we are bound by the laws of nature established by God. When (not if) the supernatural occurs in our lives, we can take no credit. It is wholly and entirely the hand of God being manifested.

Aside …

> In heaven, it's a different story. In the spirit we are not bound by the laws of nature. The only law in heaven is the law of liberty.

James 2:13-13:

So speak and so do as those who will be judged by the law of liberty. 13 For judgment is without mercy to the one who has shown no mercy. Mercy triumphs over judgment.

How does the 'law of liberty' play out here on earth? It is simply that we have liberty and so we are to show liberty to others. We've received mercy, so we show mercy. We've received forgiveness, so we should show forgiveness to other. We've received love, so we should show love. If you have trouble unconditionally showing any of these things to others, that should be a giant red flag waving before you. God is prompting you to reconnect with Him, reconnect with the source of endless mercy, forgiveness and love.

There is no secret knowledge or supernatural power obtainable by man. This idea is tied to the religious spirit. It takes focus off of the cross of Jesus Christ and puts it on our own works. Gnosticism is still around today. It is the spiritual stronghold behind secular intellectualism. It states that the key to life is obtaining more and more knowledge about God. No. The key to life is spending time with God and allowing Him to transform our nature into His and so reveal His nature to the world.

I agree with John Crowder when he states in his book 'Miracle Workers, Reformers, and the New Mystics' that 'To take hold of all the Lord has for us today, requires that we move away from a strict scholarly approach to history, to a hands on, experimental retrieval of ancient paths ways'.

1 Corinthians 4:20:
For the kingdom of God is not in word but in power.

To reduce Christianity to only an intellectual exercise is an error that has its root in Gnosticism.

Christ, the anointed one, has become for us the anointing in which we daily *'live and move and have our being'*. (Acts 17:28) As Christians we daily swim in the anointing bought and paid for by the cross of Jesus Christ. The practice of daily contemplation helps us be in tune with this reality. Seeing and being aware of God (who is all around us) and following the leading of the Holy Spirit is the goal. When such awareness starts to open itself in our lives, we see the miraculous things that God is doing all around us. He calls us to be witnesses to what we see.

For at the end of the day, our only true ministry here on earth is to be a witness to what we see.

If God shows you what He is doing, then He is calling you to witness to it. If you see the hand of God moving upon someone, go and likewise lay your hands on that person as a witness to what you see. The doctrine of 'laying on of hands' (Hebrews 6 1:2) is foundational to the Christian faith for this reason. It is a ministry of seeing and agreeing. There is power in agreement. Our power to heal or to restore as Christians is found in the power of agreement with God.

God shows us what He is doing. We lay our hands in agreement to what we see. Then, the world sees the power of God revealed in the natural and God is glorified (not us). Is this not how Jesus operated while here on earth?

John 8:38:

I speak what I have seen with My Father, and you do what you have seen with your father.

By what people saw, they knew that God was moving and that Jesus was in tune with and accepted by God. By this synchronization, they saw God's approval of Jesus' life and ministry.

But, in walking on water, they saw something more. They saw the supernatural suspension of physical law. This is something only God can do. Could God allow a created person to walk on water? Definitely! Peter walked on the water at the calling of Jesus. (Matthew 14:29) But, Peter began to sink when he took his eyes off of Jesus. This lesson demonstrates that it was Jesus enabling Peter to walk on water. It was Jesus suspending a physical law for Peter. It was Jesus. It is Jesus who is able to do this.

It is Jesus who is God.

Mount of Olives – Ascension
Acts 1:6-9:

Therefore, when they had come together, they asked Him, saying, "Lord, will You at this time restore the kingdom to Israel?" 7 And He said to them, "It is not for you to know times or seasons which the Father has put in His own authority. 8 But you shall receive power when the Holy Spirit has come upon you; and you shall be witnesses to Me in Jerusalem, and in all Judea and Samaria, and to the end of the earth."

9 Now when He had spoken these things, while they watched, He was taken up, and a cloud received Him out of their sight.

The Mount of Olives is the location where Jesus gave to us the promise of life changing power. This power would come with the Holy Spirit, the 'promise of the Father'. (Acts 1:4) Jesus promised His disciples they would do greater works than He Himself had performed. The purpose of these 'greater works' was for the Father to be glorified. (John 14:12-13) This is all to say, God wants to show His power through your life, what is stopping that from happening?

For power to flow through your life you need to have the ability to sense what God is doing around you. It is God that is moving. The key is developing your spiritual senses. You need to allow God to speak in your ear. You need to see what is happening in the spirit. You need to smell the fragrance of heaven. You need to continually taste and see that the Lord is good. (Psalm 34:8) All of these spiritual senses are developed by spending time in contemplative prayer with the Lord. (Hebrews 5:14) In your daily quiet times with the Lord allow Him to gently begin to speak and to show you things in the spirit. During your day go back to that quiet place frequently for refreshment and revelation.

Be a part of the generation who seeks the face of the Lord.

Psalm 24:3-6:

Who may ascend into the hill of the LORD?
Or who may stand in His holy place?
⁴ He who has clean hands and a pure heart,
Who has not lifted up his soul to an idol,
Nor sworn deceitfully.
⁵ He shall receive blessing from the LORD,
And righteousness from the God of his salvation.
⁶ This is Jacob, the generation of those who seek Him,
Who seek Your face.

One of the promised spiritual gifts found in 1 Corinthians is 'discerning of spirits'. (1 Corinthians 12:10) In different eras of church history, attention has focused upon particular 1 Corinthians spiritual gifts: the word of wisdom, the word of knowledge, faith, healings, miracles, prophecy, or speaking in tongues.

I believe the spiritual gift God is about to reveal in power is 'discerning of spirits'.

The word 'discernment' literally means 'to taste'. So, spiritual discernment is the ability to taste spiritually. Get into the habit of asking the Lord for spiritual direction and discernment.

The days where we speak general prayers to heal the sick are coming to an end. God wants people healed and restored. If you haven't sensed what the Lord is doing in a situation, pray and ask for discernment and then step out and pray according to what God shows you. Pray specific prayers according to what God is doing in the spirit.

It's time to return power to the church.

In the spirit, visit the Mount of Olives to receive direction from the Lord when you are about to minister to others.

From the earthly Mount of Olives, you can get a panoramic view of Jerusalem. From the heavenly Mount of Olives, you can get a panoramic view of New Jerusalem. It is from this vantage point that Jesus chose and still chooses to deliver some of His greatest teachings and insights into the ways of the spirit.

Jesus is still teaching on the Mount of Olives. Gaze in your imagination upon the New Jerusalem. Hear in your spiritual ear the wisdom of Jesus.

Opening Eyes Born Blind
John 9:1-7:

Now as Jesus passed by, He saw a man who was blind from birth. [2] And His disciples asked Him, saying, "Rabbi, who sinned, this man or his parents, that he was born blind?"

[3] Jesus answered, "Neither this man nor his parents sinned, but that the works of God should be revealed in him. [4] I must work the works of Him who sent Me while it is day; the night is coming when no one can work. [5] As long as I am in the world, I am the light of the world."

[6] When He had said these things, He spat on the ground and made clay with the saliva; and He anointed the eyes of the blind man with the clay. [7] And He said to him, "Go, wash in the pool of Siloam" (which is translated, Sent). So he went and washed, and came back seeing.

The sixth miracle that John records in his gospel is the story of Jesus giving sight to a man who was born blind. Jesus did not heal the man. Healing implies restoring to health something that has become ill. This man was born blind. He never had the ability to see at all. Jesus gave him a new ability that he had never before processed.

Jesus still has this ministry today. We all are born blind to the things of the spirit. Allow Jesus to give you your spiritual eyesight.

To receive his sight, Jesus had the man born blind go and wash in the pool of Sloam (which is translated, 'sent'). As we receive spiritual revelation by seeing into heaven, God will send to us people or send us to people who need to hear the good news: God and heaven are real and God has opened the door to heaven through the person of Jesus Christ.

Jesus is the door. He gives us access to the Father.

John 10:9:

I am the door. If anyone enters by Me, he will be saved, and will go in and out and find pasture.

I always find it amazing the man born blind, within a few hours of receiving a touch of heaven was teaching Pharisees. Pharisees were people who had spent their lifetimes studying about God. There is value in studying about God, but study doesn't compare with direct encounters with God.

The man born blind immediately offended the Pharisees.

The spirit of religion seeks conformity at all costs. Through the ages the spirit of religion has caused people to make war on others who do not conform to their particular brand of religion.

Clinging to a religious system for security is like clinging to a child's floating toy in the midst of an angry ocean. Jesus calls us to calm the sea and to walk on the water!

Religious people draw security from others doing the same thing, acting the same way, attending the same church service. They desire human validation. We need to seek only the validation that comes from God.

John 9:39-41:

And Jesus said, "For judgment I have come into this world, that those who do not see may see, and that those who see may be made blind." 40 Then some of the Pharisees who were with Him heard these words, and said to Him, "Are we blind also?" 41 Jesus said to them, "If you were blind, you would have no sin; but now you say, 'We see.' Therefore your sin remains.

I've had glimpses of heaven. My one burning desire in life is to see more. I've had touches of the Holy Spirit in my life. My one burning desire in life is to have more. None of us have arrived. We're all on a journey. I need the encouragement of others. My prayer is that I am an encouragement to you.

Mount Carmel – Victory
1 Kings 18:20-21:

So Ahab sent for all the children of Israel, and gathered the prophets together on Mount Carmel. 21 And Elijah came to all the people, and said, "How long will you falter between two opinions? If the Lord is God, follow Him; but if Baal, follow him."

Mount Carmel is a beautiful place of lush vegetation. This is why the bride groom in the Song of Solomon compares the head of his bride to Mount Carmel. (Song of Solomon 7:5)

For Mount Carmel to wither is a sign of God's wrath. (Nahum 1:4)

The prophet Elijah moved in power during his life in part because he lived on Mount Carmel. He chose to live his life continuously surrounded by the beauty of the Lord. Do you want power in your life? Spend time contemplating the beauty of Mount Carmel.

Psalm 96:6:

Honor and majesty are before Him; Strength and beauty are in His sanctuary.

Mount Carmel is also a place of victory. It is the place where the Lord through Elijah defeated the prophets of Baal. To live a victorious life, we also must spend time in the spirit in this place. We must spend time enjoying the lush slopes of our spiritual home in heavenly places. We must live in our place of victory.

I dedicate a chapter on the spiritual significance of defeating the prophets of Baal in my book 'Pathways in Heaven'.

In the contest on Mount Carmel, the prophets of Baal tried their best to persuade their god to answer. They extorted. They spent a lot of self-effort in trying to get Baal to accept their sacrifice. They leaped around their altar which they had fashioned and cut according to their tradition. They cried and cut themselves to show their zeal.

1 Kings 18:29:

And when midday was past, they prophesied until the time of the offering of the evening sacrifice. But there was no voice; no one answered, no one paid attention.

In contrast, Elijah dumped twelve buckets of water on an altar of uncut stones. He did so just to make it clear it was not by anything he had done whereby a sacrifice would be acceptable to God. No human effort, and no earthly skill is acceptable to God.

1 Kings 18:38:

Then the fire of the LORD fell and consumed the burnt sacrifice, and the wood and the stones and the dust, and it licked up the water that was in the trench.

The one and only sacrifice that has ever been or will ever be acceptable to God is the sacrifice of His only son Jesus Christ on the cross. The good news is the fact that the sacrifice of Jesus is eternally accepted by God on your behalf. It is entirely for this reason when we set aside time to spend time with God He always shows up. Not because we've 'been good' or because we sacrifice our time. It is because of the sacrifice Jesus made on our behalf.

Believe in faith God is with you. He is! Expect God to answer every prayer. He will! Do these appear to be bold and rash statements to you?

John 15:7:

If you abide in Me, and My words abide in you, you will ask what you desire, and it shall be done for you. [8] By this My Father is glorified, that you bear much fruit; so you will be My disciples.

"So you will be My disciples."

The secret is abiding. Like Elijah, learn the secret of living in a place of beauty and victory. Spend time each day on Mount Carmel. Stay in the presence of the Lord. As you do, learn to expect supernatural victory in your life. You will see victory all around you. You will see people healed. You will see the dead raised again to new life!

The Gospel is such good news the human race needed to see a redeemed life to believe it. This is the life Jesus modeled for us.

The Raising of Lazarus
John 11:1-12:

Now a certain man was sick, Lazarus of Bethany, the town of Mary and her sister Martha. ² It was that Mary who anointed the Lord with fragrant oil and wiped His feet with her hair, whose brother Lazarus was sick. ³ Therefore the sisters sent to Him, saying, "Lord, behold, he whom You love is sick."

⁴ When Jesus heard that, He said, "This sickness is not unto death, but for the glory of God, that the Son of God may be glorified through it."

⁵ Now Jesus loved Martha and her sister and Lazarus. ⁶ So, when He heard that he was sick, He stayed two more days in the place where He was. ⁷ Then after this He said to the disciples, "Let us go to Judea again."

⁸ The disciples said to Him, "Rabbi, lately the Jews sought to stone You, and are You going there again?"

⁹ Jesus answered, "Are there not twelve hours in the day? If anyone walks in the day, he does not stumble, because he sees the light of this world. ¹⁰ But if one walks in the night, he stumbles, because the light is not in him." ¹¹ These things He said, and after that He said to them, "Our friend Lazarus sleeps, but I go that I may wake him up."

Jesus raised Lazarus four days after He heard the news. Upon hearing of the death of His good friend, Jesus immediately takes the occasion to teach His disciples about having light within so as to not stumble in the night. Thomas the twin, says (in verse 16) *"Let us also go, that we may die with Him."* From Thomas' comment, we can tell that Jesus had taught His disciples not to fear death, and He Jesus, had the power over death.

Lazarus' sister Martha, who was also a disciple of Jesus, states in verse 24; *'I know that he will rise again in the resurrection at the last day.'* In response to these statements, Jesus declares in verses 25-26:

I am the resurrection and the life. He who believes in Me, though he may die, he shall live. [26] And whoever lives and believes in Me shall never die.

Do you believe this?

Much of the church is still living with the Martha understanding of resurrection and heaven, believing heaven is something waiting for us after we die. In the teaching found in John 11, Jesus dispels this notion. Heaven is right now available in His person. We are part of His body right here and now and so heaven is available right here and now. Right now, Jesus is living in the power of a resurrected life, we also right now should live our lives in the power of a resurrected life.

Having Jesus inside means having heaven inside.

Having Jesus inside means having resurrection power inside.

Moreover, those who have heaven inside are already in heaven. Heaven is not a future place to experience. Going to heaven when you die should not be a change. You should feel right at home, because it is a familiar place.

As believers we should be experiencing heaven every day. In this way physical death is nothing to fear. It simply means we are freed completely from what is tugging at us (our earthly flesh) to not enter fully.

John 11:40:

"Did I not say to you that if you would believe you would see the glory of God?"

Such an amazing statement is verse 40! Are you a believer in Jesus Christ? Do you believe that Jesus has the power over sin and death? Then Jesus is telling you that you will see the glory of God! When? Only after we die? No! That is the error reflected in Martha's and Thomas' comments. Jesus immediately corrects this error in His teaching. And later in John Chapter 14, Jesus proclaims: *"I am the way, the truth, and the life. No one comes to the Father except through Me."* (John 14:6) I AM (present tense) the truth. I AM the life. Right now you can experience Jesus, experience life, experience resurrection power, experience heaven.

This is the final of the seven miraculous lessons in the Book of John. This is where the progression of Jesus' teaches takes you, to the power of cross, to the power of the resurrection.

Summary

As a quick reference, here are the seven mountains and their associated miracles from the Gospel of John. As a contemplative prayer exercise, as the Lord directs, imagine yourself on one of the mountains; feel, taste, discern the spiritual atmosphere of each place. Slowly read the associated miracle from the Gospel of John. Allow the Lord to bring new revelation to your life.

Mount Ararat – Peace and Rest (Genesis 8:4)
Changing Water into Wine (John 2:1-11)

Mount Moriah – Sacrifice and Worship (Genesis 22:2)
Healing the Nobleman's Son (John 4:46-54)

The Mount of Beatitudes – Spiritual Eyesight (Matthew 5:1-3)
Healing at the Pool of Bethesda (John 5:1-8)

Mount Nebo – Vision and Death (Deuteronomy 32:52)
Feeding the 5000 (John 6:1-14)

Mount Sinai – Calling and Separation (Exodus 19:1-3)
Walking on Water (John 6:15-21)

Mount Carmel – Victory (1 Kings 18:20-21)
the Raising of Lazarus (John 11:1-12)

Zion, a Vision of Your Future

Zion is physically one of the seven hills upon which present day Jerusalem is built. Scripturally, the term 'Zion' represents much more. The name Zion expresses the New Jerusalem, the heavenly city and refuge being prepared for God's people. Zion is now not only our future home, but our present refuge.

The first key to entering into and experiencing Zion is sacrifice. The sacrifice acceptable to God is a broken and contrite heart. Walking humbly with God will give you entrance into Zion.

Psalm 51:17-18:

The sacrifices of God are a broken spirit,
A broken and a contrite heart—
These, O God, You will not despise.
Do good in Your good pleasure to Zion;
Build the walls of Jerusalem.

The second key is putting to death any idol worship in your life, for all idol worship must be put to death to enter Zion. All of us have idols: money, comfort, careers. None can come before God. To those who trust in the Lord and not in the security of money or property, the Lord promises to give you an abundant entrance into Zion. Be a person who daily has Zion as their refuge.

Psalm 97:7-9:

Let all be put to shame who serve carved images,
Who boast of idols.
Worship Him, all you gods.
Zion hears and is glad,
And the daughters of Judah rejoice
Because of Your judgments, O LORD.
For You, LORD, are most high above all the earth;
You are exalted far above all gods.

The inheritance of those who trust in the Lord is revelation (light) and gladness.

Psalm 97:11:

Light is sown for the righteous,
And gladness for the upright in heart.

Learn to walk humbly as a little child. Learn to have your source of joy be the Lord (and not the temporary things of this earth). Develop a heavenly mindset, where spending time in heaven with the Lord is your daily delight.

Psalm 149:2:

Let Israel rejoice in their Maker;
Let the children of Zion be joyful in their King.

Building Zion

Jesus Christ is the cornerstone of Zion, the New Jerusalem. We, as His people are being built into His Holy

City. Spend quiet time with Jesus every day. Sit with Him. Give your heart to Him. Allow His presence to change you.

Isaiah 28:16:

Behold, I lay in Zion a stone for a foundation,
A tried stone, a precious cornerstone, a sure foundation;

The makeup of Zion is not its buildings; it is its people. In a spiritual city, the buildings are directly connected to its inhabitants. In my book, 'Benches in Heaven', I describe visiting a lake-side town and how God showed me in the vision the connection between the town being built and what God was building in my life. The town directly reflected what He had done and was doing in my life, the end result being a beautiful dwelling place.

Ephesians 2:19-22:

Now, therefore, you are no longer strangers and foreigners, but fellow citizens with the saints and members of the household of God, having been built on the foundation of the apostles and prophets, Jesus Christ Himself being the chief cornerstone, in whom the whole building, being fitted together, grows into a holy temple in the Lord, in whom you also are being built together for a dwelling place of God in the Spirit.

The heavenly vision of the lake-side town has been a great encouragement to me. Through it, God revealed the fact that He is building something beautiful which will last for all eternity. Let your heart's desire become being a part of what God is building. Be a part of God's city. Know that as you seek the Lord and daily reflect Him to the world around you, you are building a permanent legacy in the lives around you.

We seek a homeland. God is preparing for us a city. On days when you are discouraged and don't see the positive influence you are having on the world around you, ask God to show you what he is building in your life, in your family, in your work, in your friends.

Hebrews 11:14-16:

For those who say such things declare plainly that they seek a homeland. And truly if they had called to mind that country from which they had come out, they would have had opportunity to return. But now they desire a better, that is, a heavenly country. Therefore God is not ashamed to be called their God, for He has prepared a city for them.

How is God building the New Jerusalem? He is doing so by perfecting those whose names are registered in heaven. His building process is going on right now. Catch the vision of what God is building in your life!

Hebrews 12:22:

But you have come to Mount Zion and to the city of the living God, the heavenly Jerusalem, to an innumerable company of angels.

We are the brick and mortar of the New Jerusalem. People think of Zion as a place to be revealed in the future. While it is true the Zion will not be fully revealed until the work of God is complete, we can right now get a glimpse of what God is building and more importantly we desperately need to have that vision.

Moses was shown a vision of the tabernacle before it was even started.

Many are looking forward to a city when the truth they need to see is they **are** the city! Many are looking to a city where God dwells. But in fact, God dwells **in them** right now! He is right now building Zion **in them**!

I Corinthians 3:9:

For we are God's fellow workers; you are God's field, you are God's building.

When this earthly body is dissolved, we have a new building of God, a house made from what God has done in and through us during this life time. Together these buildings, all made by God, all built during the lives of all the saints are being built into the holy city of God. These buildings, these city blocks, these heavenly towns are being fitly framed together into a holy dwelling place.

Why are organized churches diminishing? Structures created by human hands will never be able to hold what God is building. Denominational structures are not bad per se, but they're simply not up to the task of holding the magnificent structure God is building. The incredible structure that is the very habitation of the saints of God!

2 Corinthians 5:1:

For we know that if our earthly house, this tent, is destroyed, we have a building from God, a house not made with hands, eternal in the heavens.

Jesus is the High Priest of the incredible New Jerusalem, of the New Zion, a far greater and more perfect tabernacle. The inner sanctuary of your spirit is where Jesus right now is ministering as high priest. It is a most holy place where only the pure light of God can dwell. Walk in the light as He is in the light and you too can daily be in that place.

Hebrews 9:11:

But Christ came as High Priest of the good things to come, with the greater and more perfect tabernacle not made with hands, that is, not of this creation.

Mediate on the glimpse of the New Jerusalem found in the Book of Revelation. Notice the association of names with the construction of the city.

Revelation 21:9-12:

Come, I will show you the bride, the Lamb's wife."And he carried me away in the Spirit to a great and high mountain, and showed me the great city, the holy Jerusalem, descending out of heaven from God, having the glory of God. Her light was like a most precious stone, like a jasper stone, clear as crystal. Also she had a great and high wall with twelve gates, and twelve angels at the gates, and names written on them, which are the names of the twelve tribes of the children of Israel.

A person's name is an insight into their nature. Christians have a new hidden name which corresponds to their new nature.

Revelation 2:17:

"He who has an ear, let him hear what the Spirit says to the churches. To him who overcomes I will give some of the hidden manna to eat. And I will give him a white stone, and on the stone a new name written which no one knows except him who receives it."

When we look at a building in heaven or even the foundation of a building in heaven, we will be able to see the unique character of the person. We will see the precious gold and silver of a redeemed soul and we will continually rejoice for all eternity over God and all He has accomplished in the lives of ourselves and others.

The Lord gets excited when thinking about Zion, the joy of the future. The joy of the New Jerusalem sustained Him on His cross. He can see it. We need to see it. We need to get excited about Zion. It will shine for all eternity, declaring the wondrous works of God in and through His saints.

We need to see our part, for we all have a part. We need to see how the work God in us is the brick and mortar of buildings in Zion. We are being built into the foundations of buildings our children and their children will build upon. We ourselves have built upon the foundations of many others. Laying strong foundations, we bless those who will come after us.

To understand Zion you must perceive it, not as a city in which to live, not simply as a destination of the afterlife, but as the living body of Christ in which you are a part. Zion is being built right now in the heart and spirit of the people of God. Your part of Zion is being built right now inside of you. God is working in you to bring forth who you truly are, a child of God. Reveal God to those around you. Encourage the God working in each of them.

What is God building in the hearts of His children?

2 Peter 1:5-11:

But also for this very reason, giving all diligence, add to your faith virtue, to virtue knowledge, to knowledge self-control, to self-control perseverance, to perseverance godliness, to godliness brotherly kindness, and to brotherly kindness love. For if these things are yours and abound, you will be neither barren nor unfruitful in the knowledge of our Lord Jesus Christ. For he who lacks these things is shortsighted, even to blindness, and has forgotten that he was cleansed from his old sins.

Therefore, brethren, be even more diligent to make your call and election sure, for if you do these things you will never stumble; for so an entrance will be supplied to you abundantly into the everlasting kingdom of our Lord and Savior Jesus Christ.

God is building virtue, spiritual knowledge, temperance, patience, godliness into the hearts of His children. He wants to cure our spiritual blindness by giving us a vision of our future. God's stated goal for each of us to have an abundant entrance into the everlasting kingdom of Jesus Christ.

In Philippians Chapter 1, Paul declared (in verse 21) that *'For to me, to live is Christ, and to die is gain.'* Both Peter and Paul saw the main goal of their ministries as reminding people of the kingdom that God was building. The question is how much of the future should we expect to experience during this life here on earth? Does this physical life limit what we will experience of Zion?

Is being limited a biblical expectation or a lie from Satan meant to fool us into experiencing less than what God has for us in the here and now?

Romans 8:19-23:

For the earnest expectation of the creation eagerly waits for the revealing of the sons of God. For the creation was subjected to futility, not willingly, but because of Him who subjected it in hope; because the creation itself also will be delivered from the bondage of corruption into the glorious liberty of the children of God.

For we know that the whole creation groans and labors with birth pangs together until now. Not only that, but we also who have the firstfruits of the Spirit, even we ourselves groan within ourselves, eagerly waiting for the adoption, the redemption of our body.

The above passage from the book of Romans states that the entire created, physical realm waits for the revealing of the Sons of God. It states we currently have the *'firstfuits of the Spirit'*, but we are still waiting for the redemption of our physical bodies. (1 Corinthians 15:35-46)

Romans 8:29-30:

For whom He foreknew, He also predestined to be conformed to the image of His Son, that He might be the firstborn among many brethren. Moreover whom He predestined, these He also called; whom He called, these He also justified; and whom He justified, these He also glorified.

God's stated goal is that we be conformed to the image of His Son. To what degree can God achieve this goal in us during this life and what will be the result of the *'glorious liberty of the children of God'*?

The first thing to consider is that holiness is God's stated goal. It is God working in the hearts and minds of all believers. The only thing hindering God in this work is our willingness and desire to lay down our own selfish desires and replace them with Godly desires.

What is the goal of life? Is it to make lots of money, to be comfortable and worldly secure or is it to fully follow God and to have your security in the Lord? Money itself is not evil; it simply should not be your goal. If you make godliness your goal, God will not fail to provide for you materially. Even the Jew of the Old Testament saw prosperity as a byproduct for someone who was right with God. How much more should it be for the New Testament Christian? But, there are many kinds of prosperity and of them material prosperity is the least valuable.

Matthew 6:22:

But seek first the kingdom of God and His righteousness, and all these things shall be added to you.

Seek, pursue, make holiness your life's goal. Then, material things will take care of themselves. But, how do I do that? What does that look like? Does God want me to sit around all day praying and reading books? This was the conclusion of monks and mystics of old. However, Jesus in His High Priestly prayer in John chapter 17 prayed:

John 17:15-17:

I do not pray that You should take them out of the world, but that You should keep them from the evil one. They are not of the world, just as I am not of the world. Sanctify them by Your truth. Your word is truth.

So, the answer is not separation from the world, but to be fully engaged and yet be fully sanctified by the truth. To be sanctified means to be set apart for a holy use. To live in truth means to live in reality. Your reality as a child of God is dual citizenship.

'They are not of the world, just as I am not of the world.'

Jesus is our model to follow of what our life here on earth should look like. He is not of this world. We are not of this world. We are citizens of heaven. (Ephesians 2:19) the key to walking in this reality (your true identity) is to grow in your daily awareness of it. You do this simply by spending time every day alone with God. This is the lifestyle that Jesus modeled for His disciples.

It always seems to come back to simply spending daily time with God. Not striving. Not self-effort. The way to this life is awareness of the eternal life you have now in heaven. And that awareness is something which only comes from spending time with God.

1 Peter 2:1-10:

Therefore, laying aside all malice, all deceit, hypocrisy, envy, and all evil speaking, [2] as newborn babes, desire the pure milk of the word, that you may grow thereby, [3] if indeed you have tasted that the Lord is gracious.

[4] Coming to Him as to a living stone, rejected indeed by men, but chosen by God and precious, [5] you also, as living stones, are being built up a spiritual house, a holy priesthood, to offer up spiritual sacrifices acceptable to God through Jesus Christ. [6] Therefore it is also contained in the Scripture,

*"Behold, I lay in Zion
A chief cornerstone, elect, precious,
And he who believes on Him will by no means be put to shame."*

[7] Therefore, to you who believe, He is precious; but to those who are disobedient,

*"The stone which the builders rejected
Has become the chief cornerstone,"*

[8] and

*"A stone of stumbling
And a rock of offense."*

They stumble, being disobedient to the word, to which they also were appointed.

9 But you are a chosen generation, a royal priesthood, a holy nation, His own special people, that you may proclaim the praises of Him who called you out of darkness into His marvelous light; 10 who once were not a people but are now the people of God, who had not obtained mercy but now have obtained mercy.

All scripture quotations taken from, *Holy Bible: The New King James Version: Containing the Old and New Testaments*. Arthur Farstad, ed. Nashville: Thomas Nelson, 1982.

Made in the USA
Charleston, SC
28 August 2015